MARY AT THE CROSS

Voices from the New Testament

Loretta Miles Tollefson

Mary at the Cross © 2014, Loretta Miles Tollefson
Cover © 2014, Loretta Miles Tollefson

All Rights Reserved
LLT Press, Eagle Nest, New Mexico

ISBN-10: 0615989438
ISBN-13: 978-0615989433 (LLT Press)

All Scripture quotations are from the King James Version of the Bible

"Herodias, Salome's Mother" was originally published in *Encore, 2012*

The following poems were originally published in *Mary at the Manger,* 2005: "The Angel's Lament," "The Youngest Shepherd," "The Wise Man," "Joseph the Dreamer," "Simeon," and "Anna."

Versions of the majority of these poems, as well as the Preface, were published in *Journey of the Shunammite* by Loretta Miles Tollefson, ©2003

This book is also available in e-book format at
www.lorettamilestollefson.com

CONTENTS

PREFACE 5
JOHN THE BAPTIST'S FATHER 1
THE ANGEL'S LAMENT 3
THE YOUNGEST SHEPHERD 5
MARY AT THE MANGER 7
SIMEON 9
ANNA 11
THE WISE MAN 12
JOSEPH THE DREAMER 14
VOICE IN RAMAH 16
JOSEPH THE CARPENTER 19
JOHN THE BAPTIST 20
THE MAN ON THE BED 22
MATTHEW, TAX COLLECTOR 24
HERODIAS, SALOME'S MOTHER 26
WOMAN AT THE WELL 28
PETER'S MOTHER-IN-LAW 30
THE PHARISEE 32
THE EPILEPTIC'S FATHER 34
SIMON THE PHARISEE 35
MARY THE SISTER OF MARTHA 37
ZACCHAEUS 39
MARY AT THE CROSS 41
MARY, WAITING 43
JUDAS IN HADES 45
MARY MAGDALENE 47
AT THE TOMB 47
JESUS, RISEN 50
PETER AND HIS WIFE 52
PAUL'S THORN 56
PAUL'S JOURNEY TO ROME 58

PREFACE

No matter whether you believe the events in the Bible really happened or are "just stories," the people in those stories have much to teach us. It's easy to fall into the trap of thinking that the Bible stories aren't relevant to us today, either because we believe that the events they tell about didn't really happen or because they seem to tell us about people who had a special "in" with the Divine.

But we've all read at least one great novel or short story that helped us understand ourselves by pointing out the similarities between human beings that transcend culture and time. In the same way, the Bible stories can increase our understanding of ourselves and others. After reading these stories we can comprehend a little more clearly how even the wisest of men can justify actions of great folly. We can see why the seemingly simplest of girls can be called to enormous tasks, or what would compel a daughter-in-law to sacrifice everything to follow an old and poor woman into a land full of strangers.

And we can also see that these are men and women with human failings and strengths. They are not superhuman and thus able to experience God in a way we cannot. Nor are they less than human and in need of more-than-ordinary divine intervention. They are like us, and their link with the Divine is the same link we also can have. If they could, we can.

In the poems in this collection and in *And Then Moses Was There* I seek to ask what might it have been like to be a particular individual in a specific Bible story. How might it have felt to live those circumstances? Why might that person have reacted in that way? There are no definitive answers to these questions. Like all great literature, the stories give us clues, but not answers. Those clues provide us with a springboard for meditating on the human emotions and reactions that bridge centuries and particular habits of life, as well as on Divine grace and love, which are not bound by space and time.

The poems in this book are the result of my own meditation and research. I hope they will provide a point of departure for you, the reader, as you also "think on these things."

Loretta Miles Tollefson, March 2014

MARY AT THE CROSS

Voices from the New Testament

JOHN THE BAPTIST'S FATHER

But the angel said unto him, Fear not, Zacharias: for thy prayer is heard; and thy wife Elisabeth shall bear thee a son, and thou shalt call his name John . . . And Zacharias said unto the angel, Whereby shall I know this? for I am an old man, and my wife well stricken in years. And the angel answering said unto him, . . . And, behold, thou shalt be dumb, and not able to speak, until the day that these things shall be performed, because thou believest not my words, which shall be fulfilled in their season . . . And after those days his wife Elisabeth conceived, . . . and she brought forth a son. (Luke 1:1-57)

John the Baptist's Father

Like Zechariah of old I had looked
for the coming, but he saw more clearly
than I.

How many prophets have spoken? We
as a people had waited so long that
only the waiting had meaning. Birds
in a dark cage cannot be sent
all at once into bright light. The sun
and a fury of blind wings. Glad hope
overcome by terror
of strangeness.

The weariness of belief made me doubt. Always
events lay in the future, beyond
reality's touch. How was I to know, at that moment,
what could be true?

My heart leapt, but the mind
would not yield. Like
a long-barren woman, now blest
with small life within. Terror

of hope itself: Thoughts
refusing to grasp what
the heart already knows.
Song hovers just
out of reach, notes too fragile
to break through trembling lips.

I have had much time
for thought these past months, watching
her delight, her wonder,
and fear. The prophet
would have believed
as she has; as her cousin, who
only asked how God
would do it, did not doubt
that He would.

We old men also can learn.
The kingdom of God is upon
us, this much I
have grasped: The child
is not mine. We have
waited so long and have
so much to give,
so much to tell, but already
I know.
We cannot hold him, will not
understand all he does. I pray
God give us strength
to let him go to his future
with unclipped wings, sure
and strong in the sun.

THE ANGEL'S LAMENT

And the angel said unto them, Fear not: for, behold, I bring you good tidings of great joy, which shall be to all people. For unto you is born this day in the city of David a Saviour, which is Christ the Lord. (Luke 2:9-11)

The Angel's Lament

The human words
are so small, cannot contain
the excitement, the magnificence
of what we have
to tell them.

There will be music through the ages
that will seek to voice
this joy and yet those songs also
will be too frail
for its full weight.
No metaphor can capture
all of it. Even
the poets' lyrics fade
in wonder.

How to put into words
the dazed glory of what
is about to be? God
among them, all power poured
into such a fragile vessel,
such restricted means for grasping
the strength, the pure delight
about to enter their mortal world.
Even I can barely form the concept.
What hope for them?

I am a mind trained
to express all of God's greatness, and yet
this song bursts
through the seams
of my exultation, inexpressible
expressions pushing
at the gates of being, cascading
through my soul, no way to capture
all of it.

Ah, and He must
convey to them not only
the song, but Himself,
all in their finite terms, to their
limited hearts.

THE YOUNGEST SHEPHERD

And there were in the same country shepherds abiding in the field, keeping watch over their flock by night. And, lo, the angel of the Lord came upon them, and the glory of the Lord shone round about them: . . . And suddenly there was with the angel a multitude of the heavenly host praising God, and saying, Glory to God in the highest, and on earth peace, good will toward men. And it came to pass, as the angels were gone away from them into heaven, the shepherds said one to another, Let us now go even unto Bethlehem, and see this thing which is come to pass, . . . And they came with haste, and found Mary, and Joseph, and the babe lying in a manger. (Luke 2:8-16)

The Youngest Shepherd

I must confess that I
do not like sheep. The lambs
kick at the slightest whim, the older
ones turn away when
they should follow,
straying blindly. They must
be constantly herded, pressing
against each other's flanks, bleating
continuously, for no apparent reason.

I was only a child.
It was my first winter
on the cold hillsides, among
grown men who either
paid me no heed or teased
me unmercifully. I sat
on the outskirts
of the group by the fire.

I was warm enough that night,
next to the sleeping dogs, and tired
from a long day of following
lost lambs.

I still do not know how much I dreamed,
what I saw. I only know
the light was intense, the sound
glorious.
The men felt it too.

We left the flocks with
the dogs and groped
our way to the village, the path
uncertain in the torchlight.
By the time we reached
the stable I was wide
awake. But I saw

only a baby
asleep in a makeshift bed, the straw
poking out in all directions, its mother
smiling with tired and happy eyes, its father
hushing us
with a finger.

There was no shining light, no glory there.
And yet—long since I've had
anything to do with sheep—
still the memory haunts me.

MARY AT THE MANGER

[And the angel] said unto her, The Holy Ghost shall come upon thee, and the power of the Highest shall overshadow thee: therefore also that holy thing which shall be born of thee shall be called the Son of God. (Luke 1:35)

And it came to pass, as the angels were gone away from them into heaven, the shepherds . . . came with haste, and found Mary, and Joseph, and the babe lying in a manger . . . But Mary kept all these things, and pondered them in her heart. (Luke 2:15-19)

Mary at the Manger

My mother used to say I
was a lamb and she
the shepherd perpetually
calling me back from
wanderings for grasses no
one else could see.

I have always known
that Jehovah can do what
He pleases. That He
would use me was another
matter. The wonder
of that day still clings to my
heart as I ponder
the tiny tapering fingers,
fragile nails, wrinkled
feet, the shepherds and their tale,
the prophesies.

My thoughts are still unruly
at times, straying to
pockets of pasture so high
that the air is too
thin to sustain mortal minds.
Each day is a gift
and I the recipient
and vessel. This is
all I need to know.

I lift the baby
from his makeshift bed, breath in
his sweet milk-warmth, smooth
his fine dark hair.
Yet even while he lies curled
against my chest my
thoughts stray outward, wandering
into hidden depths,
unknown fissures in the rocks.

What does it mean?

SIMEON

And, behold, there was a man in Jerusalem, whose name was Simeon; . . . And it was revealed unto him by the Holy Ghost, that he should not see death, before he had seen the Lord's Christ. And he came by the Spirit into the temple: and when the parents brought in the child Jesus, to do for him after the custom of the law, then took he him up in his arms, and blessed God, and said, Lord, now lettest thou thy servant depart in peace.(Luke 2:25-30)

Simeon

They told me I dreamed
the impossible. Times
beyond number in these
many years I have felt
it myself—desert
of weariness.

And yet in my heart burned
a desire that would
not be denied. Certainty
at times failed me but never
the ache for fulfillment, the soul's
deepest urge toward my own
narrow path.
Compulsion or mission, who
could tell? Yet still I continued
to cling to the dream.

And now I have seen
and held in my arms the thing
that I longed for.

Many before me have dreamt
with no hope, reached
this sense of fulfillment only
in death. I have been given
it in life: my time-worn eyes gaze
on God's speaking made flesh.

I am content.

ANNA

And there was one Anna, a prophetess, . . . she was a widow of about fourscore and four years, which departed not from the temple, but served God with fastings and prayers night and day. And she coming in that instant gave thanks likewise unto the Lord, and spake of [the infant Jesus] to all them that looked for redemption in Jerusalem. (Luke 2:36-38)

Anna

> Every new baby catches
> at the heart with the promise
> they hold: parcel
> of compressed hope, a new face
> to the world. Their eyes light
> in wonder on a common
> weed and we find
> the flower
> we had forgotten.
>
> But this child—
> this child will not lose
> that fresh vision, will show
> us all, for all time
> what it is to
> truly see.

THE WISE MAN

Behold, there came wise men from the east to Jerusalem, Saying, Where is he that is born King of the Jews? for we have seen his star in the east, and are come to worship him . . . And when they were come into the house, they saw the young child with Mary his mother, and fell down, and worshipped him: and . . . they presented unto him gifts; gold, and frankincense, and myrrh. (Matthew 2:1-11)

The Wise Man

That the divine can be captured
in human form is a belief common enough.

The Attic deities, overcome with lust, making
themselves man and animal to obtain their end.
The radiant one of our own songs, bearer
of the celestial message, terror of evil spirits.

This child is somehow different. We probe
unceasingly, yet cannot touch
the thing he is—pure God, pure man entwined: must
bow before it wordlessly.

It is a painful thing for those of us
who make our living by explanations
to have no phrases complex or simple enough
to capture what lies before me now:

A tiny child who the signs have clearly shown
possesses a singular destiny, whose eyes
portend great and terrible things, whose smile
encapsulates the light. He comes

to reveal us to ourselves, lead us to power
beyond all expectation,
break open the meaning of ancient dreams,
give us God as never before.

This is all I know.
It is enough.

JOSEPH THE DREAMER

[And] the angel of the Lord appeareth to Joseph in a dream, saying, Arise, and take the young child and his mother, and flee into Egypt, and be thou there until I bring thee word: for Herod will seek the young child to destroy him. When he arose, he took the young child and his mother by night, and departed into Egypt: (Matthew 2:13-14)

Joseph the Dreamer

I am a practical man. The boards
under my hands move
obediently into place, fit
smoothly into each groove. I see
a length of wood and can say
immediately the fraction
of its cubits.

You would think a man
of my kind would
not be given to dreams. And yet
there is much that we grasp
without understanding. Slices
of conversation. Sights
the eyes acknowledged though
the heart remained silent.

While the body is motionless the inmost
mind turns over its thoughts
as a carpenter his pieces
of wood, moving the fragments
ceaselessly, holding one
against another, sanding
a corner to reveal
the true shape.

MARY AT THE CROSS

Even as I sleep the images
scatter, edges dissolving
into space, yet when
I wake, the knowledge
of what must be done comes
clear as daylight.

Loretta Miles Tollefson

VOICE IN RAMAH

Then Herod, . . . sent forth, and slew all the children that were in Bethlehem, and in all the coasts thereof, from two years old and under, according to the time which he had diligently enquired of the wise men. Then was fulfilled that which was spoken by Jeremy the prophet, saying, In Rama was there a voice heard, lamentation, and weeping, and great mourning, Rachel weeping for her children, and would not be comforted, because they are not. (Matthew 2:16-18)

Voice in Ramah

He was my firstborn child
and my last.
I who was too old
for children had conceived
by a startled husband and borne
a son.
How many times did we count
fingers and toes, touch his
chin to make him smile?
My heart sang
with unsingable joy.

In sleep he breathed
peacefulness. Awake, the house
filled with light. He began
to walk in the spring.
His delight was to explore
the edges of his world.
All work would stop as he tottered
between the doorposts, too proud
to brace himself.
My life was complete.

MARY AT THE CROSS

That morning I rose to my work
as for any other day. How
quiet it was when he slept! I paused
to consider him and pull
the blanket over his arms.
Did I worship him too much; is that
why the soldiers came?

They were there so suddenly, no knock
on the door; just
a sudden clatter
and the sword.
They had tossed his body from the bed before
I knew what was done.

And then voices.
Women who had smiled
at my child weeping
for theirs. Pile of small corpses.

There is rumor
of a child born here this time last year whose
birth was much celebrated. His parents
took him from the town
in the night, before
the indiscriminate swords.
I wish them joy.

My laughing boy lies
silent under the hot sand. No other
will take his place.

A cruel
way to welcome any
child into this world,
however precious.

JOSEPH THE CARPENTER

And it came to pass, that after three days they found [Jesus] in the temple, sitting in the midst of the doctors, both hearing them, and asking them questions. And all that heard him were astonished at his understanding and answers . . . And he went down with [Joseph and Mary] and came to Nazareth, and was subject unto them: but his mother kept all these sayings in her heart. (Luke 2:46-51)

Joseph the Carpenter

His mother broods, I know.
The words of the messenger, the tokens
of incense and myrrh.
But prophecy cannot be shredded
into meaning, must
be retained whole, with
a calm heart.
The child must remain
in God's hands.
She turns away when
I tell her these things.
I watch him
from the doorway, leaning
over his cousin, telling
a riddle.
She doesn't know how I yearn
for him also. So sweet, his clear eyes
quick to laughter or shaded
in thought. What
lies before that pure heart?
All I can do
is teach him my trade, hear
his prayers, and tell
him to go wash his hands.

Loretta Miles Tollefson

JOHN THE BAPTIST

In those days came John the Baptist, preaching in the wilderness of Judaea, And saying, Repent ye: for the kingdom of heaven is at hand . . . And the same John had his raiment of camel's hair, and a leathern girdle about his loins; and his meat was locusts and wild honey. Then went out to him Jerusalem, and all Judaea, and all the region round about Jordan, And were baptized of him in Jordan, confessing their sins. (Matthew 3:1-6)

John the Baptist

I wear the symbols of my office. Camel
> hair coat. Leathered skin, hair untouched
> by a razor.

I come from the wilderness into Jordan,
> on the path of prophets with
> the same message.

The wind blows the locust to my lips,
> the honey lies under my outstretched hand.
> God supplies me with words that will
> burn in your hearts.

You look wondering into my face,
> as if the message were a new one.
> It is not new, but it is the last.
> Time has come.

Do not weep for the sins you wash
> in the calm pools at Jordan's edge. No,
> fling your tears into the middle waters, where
> they can roll with the small stones
> to the sea.

Then give me your hands, to do a repentant
        work, and your feet to follow
        He who comes after. We shall see
        if your hearts can be made
        truly clean.

Loretta Miles Tollefson

THE MAN ON THE BED

And they come unto [Jesus], bringing one sick of the palsy, which was borne of four. And when they could not come nigh unto him for the press, they uncovered the roof where he was: and when they had broken it up, they let down the bed wherein the sick of the palsy lay. When Jesus saw their faith, he said unto the sick of the palsy, Son, thy sins be forgiven thee . . . And immediately he arose, took up the bed, and went forth before them all; (Mark 2:3-12)

The Man on the Bed

I have always been more sensitive than
other people. I
do not say it in pride. My nerves have caused
too much pain for that.
It is a sorrowful thing to goad oneself constantly.

As a child I needed no hand on my
back to know I'd done
wrong. A raised brow, a small frown would send me
to bed in tears.
Perhaps I would sleep. I could do no wrong then.

I kept to my bed until my muscles
would not obey
the simplest order. To lift my head was pain,
to walk impossible.

I knew God does not give disease without
a cause. He, who saw
my heart, had pinned me down as punishment
for all I would have
done, could I have moved.

Long hours of lying on thin mattresses
turned my eyes only
further inward. My smallest acts became
subject to a close
examination, whether tone of voice
or wrinkled brow. I
flayed myself with words, my thin hands too weak
to hold the whip.

My friends bore with me, shook their heads at my
apologies, would
not believe my pain, that I had hurt them.
It was in self-defense
they took me to the house that day, climbing
the steps eagerly,
pushing the dry rushes aside, scraping
at the hardened clay.
I wonder no one heard them.

The words of release they had gained for me
surprised them, I think.
They did not me. I felt no sense of shock
when the pebble splashed
deep in the well of my heart. I recognized
the answer when it came.

Loretta Miles Tollefson

MATTHEW, TAX COLLECTOR

And as Jesus passed forth from thence, he saw a man, named Matthew, sitting at the receipt of custom: and he saith unto him, Follow me. And he arose, and followed him. (Matthew 9:9)

Matthew, Tax Collector

How many of us choose
with full understanding what
we do with our lives? Or do we
simply drift into
a safe corner, leaves
on an intermittent wind?

How did He know what I did
not see myself? Days
of duties completed
calmly enough: dust storms
of activity blocking
the midnight doubts.

A career is like a poem, sculpted,
not planned: each piece moved
back and forth before
it finds its niche, tasks pulled
from deep within until
they fall
into their proper places.

It needs a Master's
light touch, a phrase
that drops deep into the heart, releases
the gift that was
there all along.

The recognition that day, of Him
and myself,
was overwhelming.

Loretta Miles Tollefson

HERODIAS, SALOME'S MOTHER

For Herod himself had . . . bound John in prison for Herodias' sake, . . . For John had said unto Herod, It is not lawful for thee to have thy brother's wife. Therefore Herodias . . . would have killed him; but she could not: For Herod feared John, . . . [And] Herod on his birthday made a supper to his lords, high captains, and chief estates of Galilee; And when the daughter of the said Herodias came in, and danced, and pleased Herod and them that sat with him, the king . . . sware unto her, Whatsoever thou shalt ask of me, I will give it thee, unto the half of my kingdom. And she went forth, and said unto her mother, What shall I ask? And [Herodias] said, The head of John the Baptist. And she came in straightway with haste unto the king, and asked, saying, I will that thou give me by and by in a charger the head of John the Baptist . . . And immediately the king sent an executioner, and commanded his head to be brought : (Mark 6:17-27)

Herodias, Salome's Mother

They say Cleopatra bathed
in asses' milk, as if it were
a great indulgence. I
know her action for
what it was—insurance
against time's changes, loss
of woman's power.

We have so little
to work with: our
bodies, men's desires.
The dangers are so great.
Soften for a moment,
allow a prophet or
even a child to speak, the
walls may crumble.

MARY AT THE CROSS

We use the tools at hand to
reach our ends: a sufficiency
for the time between when
men have ceased to see
our bodies and have
not yet learned to use
the craft of the agéd crone.

I have taught my daughter all
I know: her only hope in
this subservient world.
Strength of mind must be wrapped
in golden skin under
gossamer veils. Eyes bright
with paint, never pain.

She will outstrip me soon. I
see it in my husband's eyes.
My knowledge, her beauty
have gained me time. The next
step comes: a husband
for her in a sphere that
can accommodate the skills

she's so well trained in.

Loretta Miles Tollefson

WOMAN AT THE WELL

Then saith the woman of Samaria unto him, How is it that thou, being a Jew, askest drink of me, which am a woman of Samaria? . . . Jesus answered and said unto her, Whosoever drinketh of this water shall thirst again: But whosoever drinketh of the water that I shall give him shall never thirst; . . . a well of water springing up into everlasting life . . . Jesus said unto her, Thou hast well said, I have no husband: For thou hast had five husbands. (John 4:9-29)

Woman at the Well

None but my mother's spirit
could have known the number
of my husbands. She who had been
so pleased with the match
she had made for me. She died
before the beatings started.

How glad I was when he
divorced me. How little I knew
the way it would mark
all my days. The city hid me for a while.
Another man offered and I erased my stigma
in the embrace of a drunkard.
His death was a welcome relief.

And then there were the others. I had
not known there were so many ways
to feel pain.

This last is a decent man. We fled
the city together though I could not bring
myself again to say the marriage vows.
Sychar seemed a safe place.
We were not known here.

But still experience leaves its mark. The women
avoided me here as in
the alleys at home.
It is our heritage, this instinctive
shrinking from the impure.

Yet no one knew anything certain. I could
lift my head stubbornly and speak
to the men, if no one else
would meet my time-hardened eyes.
I could pretend my world was coherent enough.

Until the day a stranger at the well
offered me water
running free.

Loretta Miles Tollefson

PETER'S MOTHER-IN-LAW

Now as he walked by the sea of Galilee, he saw Simon [Peter] and Andrew his brother casting a net into the sea: for they were fishers. And Jesus said unto them, Come ye after me, and I will make you to become fishers of men. And straightway they forsook their nets, and followed him. (Mark 1:16-18)

And when Jesus was come into Peter's house, he saw his wife's mother laid, and sick of a fever. And he touched her hand, and the fever left her: and she arose, and ministered unto them. (Matthew 8:14-15)

Peter's Mother-in-Law

I have always been the proud one, unwilling
that any of mine should be found begging. When
it came time for me to go to my daughter's
house I wept in my anger.
It is our custom, yet I
made sure her husband knew I earned my keep. He
earned his too, until the preacher came.

The longer he stayed away from his nets the tighter
my lips grew. Did he think we could live
on gifts from a mob? My cooking skills ceased when
he brought his friends home. I could
not serve beggars, and told
him so. My daughter would not speak to him. She
listened to the stories as well.

Flowers, the man called us. Lambs for a father
to care for. My mind wavered and I straightened
my back. In the end all we have is our own
hands to help us. But my age

had begun to grow heavy
upon me. My head ached and my knees would not
support even these thinnest of old bones.

They say that I cried out in my fever, called
for my dead husband, wept over bread which would
not rise, beat my hands against the dark air. All
I recall is the struggle
sharp in my bones, the fury
of fear, a long barren passage dusty with
hopelessness, and the slow quiet rocking at
the end. A deep breath of peace.

I felt like a young girl as I gave them their
food that afternoon, seasoned
as I do with the herbs only these old eyes
can find on the ditch banks.

The habit of fear may assail me again;
I do not know. But my mind
was calm as the morning sea as I watched them
depart this bright morning, my
son-in-law tall in the midst of them.

Loretta Miles Tollefson

THE PHARISEE

And they come and say unto him, Why do the disciples of John and of the Pharisees fast, but thy disciples fast not?. . . And it came to pass, that he went through the corn fields on the sabbath day; and his disciples began, as they went, to pluck the ears of corn. And the Pharisees said unto him, Behold, why do they on the sabbath day that which is not lawful? (Mark 2:18-24)

And he entered again into the synagogue; and there was a man there which had a withered hand. And they watched him, whether he would heal him on the sabbath day. (Mark 3:1-2)

The Pharisee

Not to pray
and fast at the set times; to harvest
on the Sabbath; to work
a healing, however large or small, on days
of rest. What havoc
does he bring upon us?

The rules received in such
great honor so long
ago have given us
sound structure in a chaotic
world, helped to define the essence
of our lives and provided
a rope to cling to when
all was dark.

Small hands lighting candles, old
lips repeating familiar words,
women baking fragrant breads
in preparation of a sacred meal.

The rituals do often lapse
in meaning. Hands move and lips
speak with no accompanying thought.
Well I know it.
But would he have us
constantly at watch
over every thought, ready
with each heartbeat to distinguish
between our desires and God's?
Man is not made so!

All our small minds can ask
is that, as the occasion rises
and our hands reach out to touch
the sacred books, our lips
to tell the age-old words, that these
familiar motions will become
imbued, in that instant, with
the golden edge
of who we truly are.

Loretta Miles Tollefson

THE EPILEPTIC'S FATHER

And one of the multitude answered and said, Master, I have brought unto thee my son, which hath a dumb spirit; . . . And ofttimes it hath cast him into the fire, and into the waters, to destroy him: but if thou canst do any thing, have compassion on us, and help us. Jesus said unto him, If thou canst believe, all things are possible to him that believeth. And straightway the father of the child cried out, and said with tears, Lord, I believe; help thou mine unbelief. (Mark 9:17-24)

The Epileptic's Father

My heart is compressed with my lack
of understanding, pressed down
by fear of the unknown, and yet
it desires You desperately
in its limited way.

Touch me with the water of Your
word, Lord. Dissolve these chains
of my small knowledge. Let me see
You in Your glory face
to face, unblinking in the light.

Expand my heart to comprehend
Yours, if that's possible—
to grasp, at least in part, what You
are, what I can be.

SIMON THE PHARISEE

Now when the Pharisee which had bidden him saw it, he spake within himself, saying, This man, if he were a prophet, would have known who and what manner of woman this is that toucheth him: for she is a sinner . . . and [Jesus] said unto Simon, Seest thou this woman? I entered into thine house, thou gavest me no water for my feet: but she hath washed my feet with tears, and wiped them with the hairs of her head. Thou gavest me no kiss: but this woman since the time I came in hath not ceased to kiss my feet. My head with oil thou didst not anoint: but this woman hath anointed my feet with ointment. (Luke 7:39-46)

Simon the Pharisee

I had invited him, but not
as an honored guest. As one
would bid the village carpenter to come
inspect a broken table.

One does not honor
a humble man with warm water
and clean towels. He who
wanders the road is accustomed
to dust. I did not offer
amenities.

How she slipped
past the door I cannot tell.
I knew her face. Who
among us did not, except the Teacher?
The story was the usual one of great
love and sad betrayal. She
had a reputation
for doing everything
to excess.

There were tears in her eyes, but she crouched
quietly enough at the foot
of the Teacher's couch.
I did not wish to make a scene, so did
not bid her go. Too late
I saw the small stone flask she held, breathed
in the wild perfumes of India
as the drops of scented oil
slipped out one by one.
The precious liquid glided smoothly
across his dusty feet.

I bit my tongue.

MARY THE SISTER OF MARTHA

And a certain woman named Martha received him into her house. And she had a sister called Mary, which also sat at Jesus' feet, and heard his word. But Martha was cumbered about much serving, and came to him, and said, Lord, dost thou not care that my sister hath left me to serve alone? bid her therefore that she help me. And Jesus answered and said unto her, Martha, Martha, thou art careful and troubled about many things: But one thing is needful: and Mary hath chosen that good part, which shall not be taken away from her. (Luke 10:38-42)

Mary the Sister of Martha

Martha brought in another platter
as I lingered. I moved
a cup. The Master began to tell
a story. Martha came
in again and out. I moved
to the end of the table, toward
the kitchen. Peter growled a question.
The Master answered
and Matthew laughed. I brushed
a crumb from the cloth. Martha
brought in the jug of wine. Drops
spilled as I placed it. I
wiped up the spots. Martha
appeared in the doorway.
I polished the side of the pitcher
and Judas began to account
for the week's expenses. Martha
disappeared from the door. The Master
began another story and I
rearranged the bread on its platter. Martha
came in with the soup
and whispered that we needed

water for washing. I drifted
toward the door. Then Andrew
asked a question I too
had searched the answers for.
I drew closer, my hand
on the wall. John patted
the stool at his side. I shook my head, turned
toward the table. The Master
began a story about a man
from Samaria.
As he spoke I sank
down on the stool John
had offered. When the story
ended I ventured
a question of my own.
As he began to answer, my eyes strayed
to the table. The bread
was there, and the soup. The meat would soon
be ready. What else would
Martha say would be needed? I did not hear
the Master pause, only
felt his hand on my chin
as he turned
my face toward him.

ZACCHAEUS

And, behold, there was a man named Zacchaeus, which was the chief among the publicans, and he was rich. And he sought to see Jesus who he was; and could not for the press, because he was little of stature. And he ran before, and climbed up into a sycamore tree to see him: for he was to pass that way. And when Jesus came to the place, he looked up, and saw him, and said unto him, Zacchaeus, make haste, and come down; for to day I must abide at thy house. (Luke 19:2-5)

Zacchaeus

I only wanted
to see what he looked like,
this man they called honest. I had wealth
enough to be thought
important and those who
shared my ancestry crowded the pavement
but their backs formed a wall
against me. The trees
which line our streets rustled overhead.
The tall sycamore
is strong as its fruit
is sweet. The gymnasia had done
its work. I climbed quickly.
The leaves covered me. The
faces of the people were turned toward
him. He walked calmly.
A small girl clutched his hand.
He smiled at the old man at his side
and then he lifted
his head. His eyes scanned
the crowd. They stopped at the tree. Someone laughed.
I heard my name and reached
for a fig. I have heard

my name in that way many times.
Then he spoke it. The
fig fell into my hand.
I plucked another and stretched out my
arm. He took the fruit
as he looked in my eyes
and asked me to offer him welcome.

MARY AT THE CROSS

And when the days of [Mary's] purification according to the law of Moses were accomplished, they brought him to Jerusalem, to present him to the Lord . . . And to offer a sacrifice according to that which is said in the law of the Lord, A pair of turtledoves, or two young pigeons. (Luke 2:22-24)

But he was wounded for our transgressions . . . and the Lord hath laid on him the iniquity of us all . . . for the transgression of my people was he stricken. (Isaiah 53:4-8)

Now there stood by the cross of Jesus his mother. (John 19:25)

Mary at the Cross

As a baby we took
him to the temple, made
our presentation, offered
the young pigeons.
Sacrifice of praise.

As he grew we climbed
each year to the Passover, painted
the door with the young lamb's blood and gave
thanks for deliverance.

In the woman's court I stood
too far from the altar's blood to see
it, but the knowledge
was a comfort then,
and not a curse.
Symbol of dissolution, the past swept
clean. A holy thing.

And now I try to hold
within my mind the symbol that I see
before me; try not to hear
the dear-loved voice
in such great pain.
My eyelids burn, the sky
is red with grief.

There has always been a goodness
in him that could not be matched.
My pure, sweet lamb.
My quiet one.

Blood oozes from the black mark
below his bare ribs.
One pure life for us all.
The scriptures speak it.
But the sacrifice here
is not only his.

I close my eyes
and all I can see
is the hair in his face
and no hand
to brush it away.

MARY, WAITING

And, behold, there was a man named Joseph, . . . of Arimathaea . . . This man went unto Pilate, and begged the body of Jesus. And he took it down, and wrapped it in linen, and laid it in a sepulchre that was hewn in stone, wherein never man before was laid. And that day was the preparation, and the sabbath drew on. And the women . . . beheld the sepulchre, and how his body was laid. And they returned, and prepared spices and ointments; and rested the sabbath day according to the commandment. (Luke 23:50-56)

Mary, Waiting

The house is spotless but still
I cannot sleep. My grief
is not expended. Deep
into the night I pace,
the body's expression
of the heart's pain.

The spices wait for me. Gifts
I once thought were destined
for a different use. Now
they lie quietly in the small
wooden chest he carved
so lovingly so
long ago.

My mind flees
from thinking. The words,
the promises,
the pain. Even
the grinding of these spices will
be a relief, a gift
of activity.

Loretta Miles Tollefson

My thoughts will focus
on mortar and pestle, the placement
of fingers, a steady
smooth pace, not
what lies in the cave.

JUDAS IN HADES

Then Judas, which had betrayed [Jesus], . . . repented himself, and brought again the thirty pieces of silver to the chief priests and elders, Saying, I have sinned in that I have betrayed the innocent blood. And they said, What is that to us? see thou to that. And he cast down the pieces of silver in the temple, and departed, and went and hanged himself. (Matthew 27:3-5)

Judas in Hades

Even after
all this time, people ask it.
What made me do it?
Was it the greed
of silver that makes a man's
life cheap? Or was I
jealous of his
power? Did I hope to force
his hand and attain
to glory with
him? Was I a priestly spy
dissembling as I
went? Masterful
deceit! Why did I do his
bidding that night I
left the table?

I can only say it took
some time before I
found a man who
could lead me to the Council
and they no time at
all to arrange

that garden meeting. As for
the rest, I cannot
tell you. After
all this time I still do not
know what tempted me
on that gray night.

MARY MAGDALENE AT THE TOMB

And Jesus said unto her, Neither do I condemn thee: go, and sin no more. (John 8:11)

Now upon the first day of the week, very early in the morning, they came unto the sepulchre, bringing the spices which they had prepared, . . . And they found the stone rolled away from the sepulchre. And they entered in, and found not the body of the Lord Jesus. (Luke 24:1-3)

Jesus said unto her, Mary. She turned herself and said unto him, Rabboni, which is to say, Master.. . . [and] Mary Magdalene came and told the disciples. (John 20:16-18)

Mary Magdalene at the Tomb

>My name means sorrow, it has
>always been so.
>When He said to go
>and sin no more, the burden
>was only made lighter. History
>is not erased
>in a single word.
>
>A woman can train
>her face to hide
>many things.
>I always knew He
>would die untimely.
>He was too true
>to live. The cross
>was no surprise to me.

But now the tomb
is empty. I
have been inside and seen
for myself. I have run
my fingers over the rough
stone where we laid
his stiffening body. The morning light
slants gently past
the great rock they used
to block the doorway.

My chest will burst
in this vise of disbelief. The blood
rushes to my face
and my throat burns with
the effort to speak.
I close my eyes but when
they open again the tomb still
lies before me, hollow
in the sunlight.

The tomb is empty and I have seen
a vision of laughing eyes and heard
again the voice that I so foolishly thought
death would silence.

My arm is heavy.
My hand still clutches
the bundle of spices we
so carefully wrapped,
each in its package. I drink
in the clear morning air
and my hands lift

my burden to my chest. The cloth
is heavy with
the scent of perfumes
for the dead.

But the tomb contains nothing
but sunlight.
Laughter sweeps
into my arms and with a shout I fling
my bundle up, into
the trees above my head.
The tie loosens.
The small packages
begin to unravel. Sweet
and pungent smells drift
onto the breeze.

The wind clutches
my skirts. I gather
them up and begin
to run. The path is rocky
but I will not slip.
And there is no weight
strong enough to hold
me back now.

JESUS, RISEN

And [Jesus] upbraided them with their unbelief and hardness of heart, because they believed not them which had seen him after he was risen. (Mark 16:14)

Jesus saith unto him, Thomas, because thou hast seen me, thou hast believed: blessed are they that have not seen, and yet have believed. (John 20:29)

Jesus, Risen

There has been so much blood spilled over
the ages. As if reducing a life
to its bodily fluids will propel
us beyond our own limitations. As
if we are only the dust our bodies
are made of. As if the power in my
captured hand was truly subject to your
tightening fingers. As if your yowls for
my blood were not only lust for a break
in the fence of limitation, but terror
of it as well.

You put so much stock in blood: its wetness,
its stickiness, its smell. You forget. It too
is mere substance: result of life, not life
itself. You know instinctively that you are not
all you appear. As I am not.
But limitation binds the mind so tightly
that you cannot imagine life exists
in any other form. Yet, I tell you,
the rough ropes will unravel wildly

in the instant you recognize why "heart"
serves as metaphor for "soul." It is not just
a muscle, or clutch of emotion. It's a symbol
of more than mere blood. I stand before
you now, drained of all apparent substance.
Limitation has not destroyed me.

Are you listening?

Loretta Miles Tollefson

PETER AND HIS WIFE

Another parable put [Jesus] forth unto them, saying, The kingdom of heaven is likened unto a man which sowed good seed in his field: But while men slept, his enemy came and sowed tares among the wheat, and went his way. . . . But he said, . . . Let both grow together until the harvest: and in the time of harvest I will say to the reapers, Gather ye together first the tares, and bind them in bundles to burn them: but gather the wheat into my barn.(Matthew 13:24-30)

And when the disciples saw him walking on the sea, they were troubled, saying, It is a spirit; and they cried out for fear . . . [But Peter] walked on the water, to go to Jesus. But when he saw the wind boisterous, he was afraid; and beginning to sink, he cried, saying, Lord, save me. (Matthew 14:26-30)

And [Jesus] was transfigured before them. And his raiment became shining, exceeding white as snow; . . . And Peter answered and said to Jesus, . . . let us make three tabernacles; one for thee, and one for Moses, and one for Elias. For he wist not what to say; for they were sore afraid. (Mark 9:2-6)

And Peter remembered the word of Jesus, which said unto him, Before the cock crow, thou shalt deny me thrice. And he went out, and wept bitterly. (Matthew 26:73-75)

But Peter, standing up with the eleven, lifted up his voice, and said unto them, . . . Repent, and be baptized every one of you . . . And with many other words did he testify and exhort, . . . the same day there were added unto them about three thousand souls. (Acts 2:14-41)

Peter and His Wife

Where do the words begin? The heart
has many chambers, each
mysterious in its
own way. The Spirit
speaks, or is it me?
What moves these lips?

MARY AT THE CROSS

He has the purest heart
of anyone I know.
The words
gush out, unchecked
by anything but
the emotion they contain.

Tares and wheat rise
steadily, the shoots
young and difficult
for my green eyes
to differentiate.
My heart burns with pain.

His is a heart to trust implicitly.
Clear water, the shadows
on each stone: The depths
are all laid bare.
It is a glorious
and a frightening thing.

What does it mean to speak
in Spirit, no barrier between?
I say what is so deep
within as to be undefined
until the words are formed.

A look of recognition, a nod:
I know I have hit home.
Ah the giddiness. And yet
the next phrase brings
only laughter.

*The pain he suffers sears
my heart and yet my hands
remain empty of help
for him. He paces the floor
and I have nothing
to offer but
my love.*

How am I to know what
is right, what wrong, Spirit
or not?
Where does certainty come from?
I search my heart, His face.
My ears burn with shame.
And then
I see Him smile.
Ah, time
and growth, the sun of His love,
the liquid of His words. These
are the healing power.

*Patience has never been
his strong point. He conquered
my heart in a whirl of urgent words, and now
he must stand still,
be silent.
He was already perfect
in my eyes—that loving
and that stormy heart—but now
I see a man I had
not dreamed of: Miracle
of growth.*

The cloudy waters, the mist
on the mirror
will clear with time.
Young plants full grown display
their strong true colors, sharp
tassels of fruit.
Then I will know when
I speak true, when false.
Then the weeds will come
out swiftly.

I pray for courage as I wait
beside his hungry soul. Wisdom
to speak and
to be still, a quiet
trusting mind. This
is a man to blaze
a glorious path, when he
has reached full height, when
his heart has found
all that it seeks.
I pray God
give me strength.

PAUL'S THORN

There was given to me a thorn in the flesh, the messenger of Satan to buffet me, lest I should be exalted above measure. For this thing I besought the Lord thrice, that it might depart from me. And he said unto me, My grace is sufficient for thee: for my strength is made perfect in weakness. (II Corinthians 12:7-9)

Paul's Thorn

Great deeds are not done
in a vacuum. They leave
their mark on the soul. As do
the deeds of the heart:
struggle fierce
as any battle. And
leaving its sign.

The glory of it
—God's face, the transcendence.
A bright flame and a wholeness.
The earth seemed very
dim, afterwards. I could
have stayed always
in that bright light. Pain
brought me back. The vessel
is weak and will burst
under pressure.

So Jacob must have
felt as that gray morning
of uncertainty dawned. The
angelic struggle
had freed his soul, but not
his body.

MARY AT THE CROSS

Jacob, the ache in the thigh
slowing his progress,
giving him time to reflect.
I, this thorn ever digging,
widening its circle
of pain, finding new points
for the pressure: unending
humanness.

Loretta Miles Tollefson

PAUL'S JOURNEY TO ROME

And [Paul] said unto them, Sirs, I perceive that this voyage will be with hurt and much damage, not only of the lading and ship, but also of our lives. Nevertheless the centurion believed the master and the owner of the ship, more than those things which were spoken by Paul . . . And when neither sun nor stars in many days appeared, and no small tempest lay on us, all hope that we should be saved was then taken away . . . And the soldiers' counsel was to kill the prisoners, lest any of them should swim out, and escape. But the centurion, willing to save Paul, kept them from their purpose; . . . And so it came to pass, that they escaped all safe to land. (Acts 27:1-44)

And so we went toward Rome. And from thence, when the brethren heard of us, they came to meet us as far as Appii forum, and The three taverns: whom when Paul saw, he thanked God, and took courage. (Acts 28:14-15)

Paul's Journey to Rome

It had been a long journey.

The centurion was a good man but hard,
the brick of his knowledge more real
than experience itself.
Pat me on the shoulder as a man
would a child. Willing
to accommodate but not listen
to the experience of age
or, heaven forbid,
the voice of God.

Many times a friend, always
a stranger.
Did he think me mad,

spouting strong words with no meaning?
Even the captain and men: only
fear of death made them listen.

Until the danger was past. Faith
born of terror is a piece
of frail cloth that blows
away in the breeze
of a clear sunny morning. Oh

to be among a people who had heard
of the hearing, the comfort of speaking
to eyes that were not dazed
with disinterest or dazzled
by marvels. What

lay ahead? Would they all be slow
to hear, quick to forget? Birds circling
above the grain, whirling
away again from the stripped field?
Quicksand of greed's memory.

Minds hard as Rome's roads and bridges
of concrete. Stiff as the letters that form our heavy,
stable words. Citizen
though I am, still
the East has its impact.
There's much to be said for dust
underfoot, moving softly aside, cushioning
the jar of one's thoughts.

Loretta Miles Tollefson

These blocks of gray stone lie inert, do not
respond to a softer or firmer step,
do not turn for a green fertile field
or proud but small stream.

Straight and unseeing we marched forward.
My eyes too began to see nothing
but the dull stones underfoot.

And then the Forum and the three taverns.
Crowds of faces eager
and anxious and glad.
How my heart lifted as I raised
my old head to their gaze.

www.ingramcontent.com/pod-product-compliance
Lightning Source LLC
Chambersburg PA
CBHW071414290426
44108CB00014B/1822